Why Are My Nuts in the Toilet Water?

And Other Questions Older Men Need Answered.

Allen F. Mahon

Allen F. Mahon

Why are My Nuts in the Toilet Water?

Copyright © 2015 Allen F. Mahon

Stephen, Donovan & Carson Publishing

ISBN: 1519120745
ISBN-13: 978-1519120748

Other books by Allen F. Mahon

Embraced by Angels
Gone Home for Angels
The Siler Saga
Soap Making Essentials

DEDICATION

This book is dedicated to my aging body. I wouldn't be here without it.

Why are My Nuts in the Toilet Water?

THIS BOOK IS PRINTED
IN LARGE PRINT FOR
ITS TARGET AUDIENCE.

FOR OBVIOUS REASONS.

Why are my nuts in the toilet water?

Gravity, plain and simple. Older men have the same issue women have as they grow older, only our issue is lower on the body. If you wear briefs you may not notice this phenomenon of drooping twins until your pair come in contact with something startling, like a cold, wet encounter in the bathroom. My first encounter nearly caused me to jump up off of the john. If you wear boxers you may have an earlier warning as the twins creep down the inside of your leg over time. Unfortunately there is no good solution for this condition. You can skootch forward and try to rest them on the front rim of the toilet seat. This doesn't always work as the rim may be cold or it can also be slippery, causing the boys to fall back down and into the water, sometimes causing a splash. Using a wash cloth, a nearby magazine or a bunch of wadded up toilet paper strategically placed between the boys and the rim may be a solution here. The other possible solution is to physically hold them up out of the water with your hand.

I am currently working on a type of net to keep them dry. I haven't figured out if it should be hooked to the toilet seat or to the upper thighs. Oh well, I'll let you know when and if I get the design worked out. I will most likely sell it on TV with an infomercial. I'll call it something like the "Nut Nest" and sell it for $14.99 plus $5.99 shipping. If you order within a limited time I will throw in a second "Nut Nest" for free. You just pay $5.99 additional shipping. That would be a pair of "Nut Nests" for your pair.

Why is there hair growing where I don't want it?

This is a great question! If you figure it out, let me know. I was in my mid-fifties and woke up one morning to what felt like a three foot hair growing out of my left ear. In the course of six months it was numerous, thick, dark and coming out of both ears. It was not only on the inside but also growing on that little piece of your ear that looks like a lid to the ear hole but isn't really a lid to your ear hole. It acts more like a baffle unless you push in on it, then it is more like a lid. Sorry, what was I saying? Oh yes; I also get a few on the ear lobe. The odd thing is I always have about twice as many in my left ear as I do in my right ear.

I asked my barber one day why this was happening to me. His answer was pretty lame. He said we all have those hairs but when we get older they thicken and grow longer. He was a good barber. So maybe he was right, I have no clue. He also offered to trim them as a free service. I checked his ears and yup, he has hair there too.

Now, let's talk about nose hair. What the heck is that all about? They just appeared one morning like the ear hairs. They stick out beyond the end of your nostrils and move about as you breathe. I have a full beard and mustache. This compounds the issue. When the nose hairs get too long they sometimes come in contact with the moustache hairs and cause a tickling in the nose. This can lead to a sneeze or a rubbing of the nose with your hand. Neither one is very attractive. And trust me, your wife will let you know about it.

Eye brows are the other place that you will wind up fighting hairs. These fellows are already there. You already knew they were there. They too, will become uncontrollable. It's like the fertilizer gnomes come in the middle of the night and spread 10-10-10 on your eye brows. The hairs will grow like you wish your tomatoes grew.

There are some measures you can take to get rid of all of these unwanted pests. You can get a pair of scissors designed to cut these hairs. They are very small and I have thick fingers and hands. Getting my sausage like appendages in those scissor holes was like trying to fit a watermelon through a garden hose. They even make an electric trimmer, plug in or battery operated, to do the cutting quickly. I have tried them both with some success. The humming and vibration was kind of nice. Then there is waxing. Never tried it. If you are brave enough, go for it. The last alternative is pulling them out. This also works but just like the other methods, the hairs will always come back and bring more of their friends and relatives with them. Please, whatever you do, NEVER, EVER, under any circumstances, pluck your nose hairs!

Women have their own devices and lotions and stuff designed to get rid of hair. I wouldn't recommend the lotions as I would think putting that stuff up your nose could cause brain damage just from the fumes alone.

Why does everything I eat and drink turn to gas?

When I was a young man I could eat anything and everything. I never had a problem with my stomach or bowels. Lately, EVERYTHING I eat or drink gives me gas, both upper gas and lower gas. Belching and farting have become commonplace.

Lately I have been cutting back on my food intake in an attempt to lose weight. I still have the same amount of gas. I stopped drinking carbonated beverages… still have gas. Stopped eating spicy foods… still have gas. No vegetables like cabbage, broccoli and other members of the plant fart family… GAS!

When you can't beat a problem like this, the only alternative is to embrace it. So I gave up trying to figure it out and am just careful where and when I allow a pressure release to happen. Being an author and working at home all day allows for free form gas release. I just keep plenty of air fresheners on hand. That explains why you will see those little pine trees hanging from my office ceiling fan.

Why does my body make all those strange noises?

I am talking about LOUD noises! My knees, hips and ankles Snap, Crackle and Pop more than breakfast cereal. You would think I had bubble wrap shoved down both legs of my pants and somehow my body's lower half was popping the bubbles as I walk.

There are gurgling and blurp-ping sounds coming from my stomach and intestines. This happens when I am hungry or when I have just eaten a big meal or a snack or had a sip of water; oh, HELL it happens all of the time. (see the previous question about gas).

The upper half of my body is not very quiet either. Shoulders, elbows, wrists, knuckles, neck and even my jaw sometimes pops! Some days I feel like I should go down to "Happy Lube" and have them put me on the RACK.

What is up with skin tags? And while we are on the subject, just what the HELL is a "Skin Tag"?

OK, I went to the internet and looked this one up. They just happen! What! The internet said they can happen to anyone, especially people who are overweight. I am a few pounds over my ideal weight. I have had one or two of them at the base of my neck and one pesky one in my left arm pit. The ones on my neck were small but the one in the armpit, OH MY GOD! It looked like I was growing a third arm!

They are nothing more than benign lumps of skin that grow out of your normal skin at random. They cause little discomfort unless they are in the way when you shave or if they get irritated by your clothes rubbing on them, case in point, my underarm one.

They appear in strange places, at the base of the neck (me), in your arm pit (also me), under your breast, around the crotch area and my favorite… in the creases on your buttocks. What the… in the creases of your buttocks? Really?

Do not try this! I cannot say this enough, <u>DO NOT TRY THIS</u>! I cut the one under my arm off by myself. Yes, I did. It hurt like I don't know what! It also bled. Not just a few drops… IT BLED! You would think

I cut a main artery. It was a couple of weeks before I could take off the bandages for good. On the bright side, it didn't come back.

Why do I have trouble with my weight?

Actually, I don't have a problem with my weight. My doctor has the problem. Yes, I am a pound or twenty over the ideal weight for my height and age that *"they"* say I should be. Come on, I'm not as active as I once was. The calories don't burn off as quickly. Time was, I could lose three pounds just by going to the bathroom. Get up, walk to the fridge for a snack; two pounds gone. Eat the snack I just got from the fridge; one pound lighter. Now, if I think about one doughnut I gain weight!

My doctor says it's my slower metabolism. If my metabolism is slower, then why is my heart rate faster?

Why do women of all ages smile and say hello to me?

Now this one is a killer. Since my hair turned gray, I put on a couple of pounds and my face shows more wrinkles, women, of ALL ages, races and types are saying hello and smiling at me wherever and whenever I go in public. It happens at the grocery store, in restaurants or pretty much anywhere. I am serious here! Where were they when I was young and single. My wife says it's because I am old, chubby, harmless and cute. She says they look at me and see a harmless grandpa. I'm not buying that. I still like to think I'm a bit dangerous and edgy.

Edgy?

No?

A little rough around the edges perhaps?

No?

Oh, hell, she is probably right!

Why am I getting shorter?

I am five feet eight inches tall. That is not tall nor is it short. It is right around average. Since high school I have been five feet eight inches. In the military they measured me at five feet eight inches. I have government documents to prove it.

I go for a checkup at the doctor's office. They have me stand with my back against the wall where they have inches and feet marked on a vertical chart. "Five feet, six and one half inches," the nurse says. WHAT! Are you kidding me? I tell her to look at my chart from my last visit. She does and says I was five feet eight then but five feet six and one half now. This is crazy! I look at the measurements on the wall to see if they are off. I also inspect the floor where I was standing and tell her there appears to be a slight dip in the tiles. She puts me on the scale and pulls that metal bar thingy up and swivels a flat piece on my head. I stand as tall as I can, because now I am worried. "Five feet seven," she announces. Well, good, there is at least one half inch I got back. I knew that floor had a dip in it.

At this point I let it go. A month or two later I go to my chiropractor. He does the adjustment thing and I feel great. I also bring up the height thing. He tells me that because my back was out of whack, my discs were compressed. He claims that the adjustments he just made opened them back up. To prove it he takes me back to his scale and does the same measurement routine the nurse did to me. "Five feet EIGHT inches," he says. So all this time that pesky inch was hiding at the chiropractor's office!

I drove immediately to my doctor's office and ran inside. I found his nurse and demanded she measure my height. She refused at first without an appointment, until I explained the whole situation to her. She remembered what happened and told me they all shared a good laugh at my expense. Was she ever surprised when she measured me at...

<u>FIVE FEET EIGHT INCHES!</u>

Why do I grunt when I get up?

When I get up from a sitting or squatting position I grunt like a weight lifter. When I sit or squat down, I grunt like I am giving birth. When I swing my legs out of bed in the morning, I grunt. When I pick anything up, even as light as an egg, I grunt. Open a door, grunt. Up or down stairs, grunt. No matter what the occasion, I have an appropriate grunt. My favorite grunt is the one followed by a sigh.
GRUNT - AHHHH!

Why does my wife not hear 80% of what I say lately?

Lately, I have been talking to my wife, telling her about my day or sharing something I heard or experienced and noticed she is reading, watching TV of checking her email. I will ask her if she is listening to me and I always get a "Sure". Sometimes I will ask her what she thinks about what I just said and she asks me to repeat my story. It gets very frustrating having to say things twice or even three times!

Wait! I think she has been doing this since before we were married. I just can't remember.

Why do I repeat myself?
Why do I repeat myself?

See the previous question!

After thoughts

I know this book didn't answer most (or any) of the questions posed but I hope it kept you entertained. Trust me, if I knew the answers, I would be rich. Seriously I think the real question is not why these things happen to us but how are we going to deal with them when they do happen. Aging is inevitable. We just need to deal with all that aging throws at us with dignity, grace and a good sense of humor.

ABOUT THE AUTHOR

Allen Mahon lives and continues to age in Buchanan, Virginia with his wife, Randee and his dog, Charlie. He is retired from a career in the IT industry and devotes most of his time writing (serious) novels and pondering the workings of the Universe and of his body.

Made in the USA
Coppell, TX
16 October 2022

84649776R00021